CW01481375

Written by Mia Rose
Cover Design by Mia Rose
Illustrations by Mia Rose
Brush Lettering by Mia Rose

Printed in the United Kingdom

ISBN: 978-1-521-40369-3
First Edition, 2017

4th Floor, Regus House
4-12 Regent Street
SW1Y 4RG

Email the Author at: info@kryptikrose.com
Visit the Author's Brand at: www.kryptikrose.com

#FBLOGGER

TWENTY SECRETS TO FASHION BLOGGING &
ATTRACTING BRANDS TO YOU

Written, Illustrated and Lettered by
Mia Rose

For the only rose in my life, my mother. You inspire me to be the best version of myself.

KryptikRose™

KryptikRose™, a London based indie brand, is my brain child. Hi! My name is Mia and I am a fashion, design and Pop Art enthusiast, and dare I say it, also a fierce millennial girl boss. I have always found vibrant colours, patterns and textures absolutely fascinating. This aesthetic reflects in the clothing and accessories I design for KR™, as well as other products I curate into my brand. The world is full of boring clothes and accessories; KryptikRose™ is about bringing smiles to the faces of those who wear KR™, and also to those who don't!

I plan to eventually bring KryptikRose™ to your nearest mall, so that you can escape the realities of life and indulge in the alternative aesthetic of colour and fun. All in good time!

Who is Mia?

I am a twenty-something boss babe and/or female entrepreneur. I've been working for myself since I was 21 years old. After pursuing my Undergraduate degree in *Art, Design and Media*, I pursued a freelance career in Graphic Design for 5 years. I learned the ropes of running a business myself fairly quickly, but gained more insight through attaining two Masters Degrees; one in *Marketing Communications* and the second in *Management and Leadership*.

Somewhere along the line, I realised that corporate design didn't give me the creative freedom I was craving for. In the back of my mind, yearnings of wanting to get into fashion kept creeping up, but the opportunity never presented itself, until 2012. I chose to write a Business Plan for my final Masters Dissertation for a potential fashion brand.

This allowed me to measure the possibility of merging Graphic Design with Fashion without abandoning my existing career altogether. My careful planning proved fruitful eventually and the rest is history! KryptikRose™ was officially launched in 2014 and caters to an international market.

Thankfully, KryptikRose™ customers enjoy my creative and colourful fusion of my artwork on tops and accessories like bags and phone cases. Inspired by Pop Art, my aesthetic is definitely a treat for the senses.

To visit the brands website, log on to: www.kryptikrose.com

Other places to find us:
Twitter: @kryptikrose_ldn
Instagram: @kryptikrose_ldn
Pinterest: @kryptikrose_ldn
Facebook: Kryptik Rose

Hold on Mia...

So, why write this book?

Now that you know a little bit about who I am, you most definitely are wondering why an owner of a fashion brand is writing a self-help book for fashion bloggers (#fbloggers). Well the answer is simple. Along the way, having two businesses under my belt and #fblogging myself, I learned a lot of valuable information that will be useful for a number of aspiring entrepreneurs and fashionistas. Working for yourself forces you to constantly learn, but there comes a time when you want to share the wealth of knowledge you have acquired. This is where this book comes in.

Understanding the struggles of making my own businesses a success, I am truly empathetic to anyone who wishes to earn a living by working for themselves and being their own boss. And when you've just started out, it can be really difficult without any guidance.

I have found that trial and error is the best way to generate the most effective formulas of success, as I too am a #fblogger. As a brand I've worked with and continue to work with a range of #fbloggers. And as a business, I have worked very hard to create a friendly relationship between the brand, KryptikRose™ itself, and the fashion bloggers I have worked with. One of my greatest efforts alongside running my own fashion brand is to use KR™ as a platform to encourage and build aspiring fashion bloggers that would otherwise be over looked.

Many #fbloggers that have worked with KR™ have found their images being published in fashion magazines like

Cosmopolitan, *VOGUE*; and this opens up new avenues for them.

This book will talk about how to start your journey as a #fblogger, what to expect on said journey and highlight the etiquettes of working with a brand; big or small.

Being a fierce girl boss, I feel I must be a mentor for aspiring girl bosses. I am thinking about writing a series of books, and the first one just happens to help fashionistas. I hope you, my dear reader, find this book helpful in your journey ahead.

I would love to hear from you, so do get in touch with me on Twitter: @thekryptikrose. Alternatively, you can email with any questions at: info@kryptikrose.com

designer
BRANDING
FASHIONISTA
streetwear
#FBlogger
POST
styling
style
celebrity
blogger
#fblchat
vlogging
fashion
haul
what I'm wearing
#OUTFIT
contest
INSTAGRAM
fashion blogger
H&M
clothing haul
milan fashion week
LONDON FASHION WEEK - LFW
street wear
FASHION
youtube
lookbook
network
Chanel #5
#FOTD
COSMO
#FBlogger
fashion
diy
SOHO
FACEBOOK
collab
nyfw
TOPSHOP
review products
guest blog
WORDPRESS
#beechat
highstreet
#MCM
jewellery
STREET
#OOTD
affiliate
beauty
OXFORD STREET
snapchat
style
Saatchi Gallery
LONDON FASHION WEEKEND
BLOGGER TWITTER CHAT
#OOTN
kryptik rose
BLOGSPOT
STREET STYLE
digi cam
somerset house
MEDIA KIT
my favourites this month
ambassador
CANON
shop my style
success
LIVE STREAM
blogginggals
couture
fashion blogger
VOGUE
#WCW
macbook
depop
SOCIAL MEDIA
periscope
catwalk
GIVEAWAY
COLLAB
magazine
facebook live
photoshoot
trendsetter

f•blog•ger (noun)
(ef-blawg-er)

1. An individual who blogs about fashion; alternatively referred to as a *fashion blogger*
2. A fierce fashionista who writes about fashion; male or female

did I save that #fblog last night?!?
I need to write a review!
take pics for that blog post!
Reply back to KryptikRose™ about our collaboration!
aaah! what time was that Twitter chat?!
need to get some props for the photoshoot!
edit the haul video I shot yesterday!
tap tap tap tap tap
RIVER ISLAN
H&M
CHANEL
need to create my lookbook for this season today!
what products am I loving this month?
what should I wear to the Blogger event?!
Need to buy tickets for London Fashion Week!
ummm... wait... have I eaten today?!
sleep? hah! who needs sleep? *yawn*
I've hit a road block but I need this #fblog post out today!!!

1st Secret

Take it Seriously...
But not TOO serious!

"*our intention creates our reality*"

— WAYNE DYER

I

Blog with Intention

For anything to be successful, you need to have the intention of making it work. If you want your project; whatever it may be, to be successful, you have to at some point take it seriously in order to build the foundation. Once the foundation has been built, you can truly start to enjoy the process as well as bear the fruits of your success. Determine whether it is something you want to do full time, or as a "side hustle". More often than not, it is wiser to start any business adventure off as something on the side. It helps you determine whether the direction is worth taking, whilst keeping a source of income open. If and when you start making serious money from your "side hustle", you then give up the "side" and it becomes your "main hustle"!

"if you want TO BE original, BE READY TO BE copied"

— COCO CHANEL

2nd Secret

Be original...

"no niche is too small if it's" — SETH GODIN

2

Find your Niche

There are literally thousands upon thousands of fashion blogs (#fblogs) all over the world. Every country is bursting with budding fashionistas looking to make a mark. On occassion, there are girls who just start a fashion blog for the sake of it. They are so easy to spot out because there is no thought into the design or voice. It's extremely important to be original in such an already saturated field of #fblogging. It's difficult to be found, but not impossible.

Decide which sector within #fblogging you want to write in. Is it street fashion, high fashion (where all you talk about are designer and luxury brands), high street fashion, DIY, fashion and lifestyle etc. Maybe you choose a hybrid of fashion, sportswear, health and fitness. The options can be literally endless if you really narrow down what *your* interests are. As long as you are interested, you won't have such a hard time creating the necessary content.

The world may seem lonely sometimes, but the great thing is, it isn't and there will most probably be an audience for what you want to put out. Put out a few feelers and you should start to understand which direction you need to head in.

Bottom line is, find your niche and run with it.

3

Know Your Audience

The next step is figuring out who your demographic is going to be; this includes, but is not limited to their gender, their location as well as their age. Where do they like to shop? What do they like to buy? Who are their celebrity influences?

Knowing your audience allows you to further develop and narrow down your niche. By understanding who exactly your readers are, you will be able to create content that is fun and interesting for you to produce, but you will know you're not wasting your time creating it, since they will enjoy reading your #fblog. Determining your target market also helps in deciding which brands you want to work with in the near future. If you have a random selection of different types of brands on your #fblog, it just comes across as haphazard and painfully clear that you are not sure of what you want nor are you entirely sure of what you can deliver. Often times, brands will be willing to work with a fairly new #fblogger, as long as their "shop front" (your fashion blog) shows you mean business.

Don't be afraid to refuse to work with brands that don't fit your niche. If they have nothing to do with what you write about, it can hurt you more than help you. So be mindful of this and make sure the brands you work with fit in with your niche.

3rd Secret

As a #fblogger, you ARE your brand

"design is the
SECRET AMBASSADOR
of your
BRAND"

—PAUL RAND

4

Create a Brand

Branding is extremely essential if you want to be a #fblogger that stands out from the crowd. It shows you're serious about what you're doing and won't waste anyone's time; especially brands. Even if you're a completely brand new #fblogger, a striking brand is the stepping stone to success and being noticed! If you're looking to make this a career, or even as "after hours", look into hiring a graphic designer if you're not too artistically inclined. Work towards creating a brand and a "store front", your website, that is true to who *you* are and who you want the fashion world to see. Take your time and don't rush things.

Some of the things to consider when putting your brand together is (1) the name of your

#fblog. Make sure it is something you won't regret a few years down the line and is URL friendly. Common phrases and words are almost always taken, so keep the name unique. Your name should be available on all Social Media (SM) platforms you want to be on, and should be the same throughout so that your readers can find you easily. I'll be going into more detail about SM later on in the book.

Once you have decided on a name, think about how you want the name represented; (2) think about your brand logo. Will it be an image or a playful or iconic typeface. If you have design experience, great, otherwise don't hesitate to hire a Graphic Designer to create a logo for your brand. This may require an initial investment, but believe me, it will help you in the long run; especially if this is something you are serious about pursuing as a full time career. Even if you don't want an illustrative logo, it is always better to get some design advice for your logo from a professional. Maybe you have a friend who is a Graphic Designer who can give you advice for free! Even if you are surrounded by family and friends who are not in the creative sector, ask for their opinion. It is always helpful to understand how others respond to the name and logo of your brand. So don't be shy to ask your mum for advice either! Sometimes the aesthetic we are trying to put across doesn't always translate well to others. So, always get opinions.

Right, you have the name and logo decided, now what? This is when you need to determine what your website is going to look like. (3) Brainstorm and finalise the colour scheme of your website; these colours will be in harmony to any used in your logo. If it is a grayscale logo, then you have free reign on what colours you can potentially use throughout your #fblog. But one thing is very important; *colour harmony*. Make sure the colours you use are those you won't get tired of easily, nor will your readers. Make sure you don't go for pale yellows as they almost never translate well on the screen, unless they are used against a dark background. After deciding your colour scheme, you are now ready for one of the most important parts of your blogging journey, (4) designing your #fblog. Many girls choose to take this task on to themselves because websites like Wordpress and Blogspot have relatively easy interfaces that allow you to set up your #fblog with a certain theme very easily. If you are looking for a more specialised and bespoke #fblog interface, this is where you should seek a Web Designer, if you are wanting to go the extra mile in the beginning. You can always revamp your #fblog once you realise you have a knack for this and are actually engaging an audience. But the more prep work you do in the beginning, the more time, money and effort you save yourself in the long run. It just depends on how you choose to approach things.

(5) Another aspect of branding you will need to consider is whether you choose to blog anonymously or whether you want people to know the real you. What I mean by this is, do you share pictures of yourself in your work, or do you keep your identity concealed and allow the products you review and your creativity to speak for itself. Maybe you want to create a persona that is industry specific. This way, you get to maintain some privacy, whilst being out there. This gives you control on how much personal information your readers gets to know about you. Sometimes, audiences can get carried away with wanting to know every last detail of your life; something we can very evidently see when it comes to *YouTubers*. They choose to share a

massive chunk of their lives, or at least that is how they present their work. After years of this, some end up regretting it and go radio silent. As a #fblogger, you have a choice. Make it wisely.

One of the last things in branding is taking your fashion blog branding from screen to paper. (6) It is always helpful to have a set of business cards printed for yourself that you can always keep handy. They will be especially helpful when you go for networking or places like *Fashion Week* or other such events. Make sure you have your name, the URL link to your #fblog and at least one way you can be contacted on your Business Cards.

These are just some of the most important aspects of branding every fashion blogger must take into consideration if they are serious about this venture; whether it be a "side hustle" or a full time gig.

4th Secret

"Ideas are the most valuable thing...
Curation is that means to the end."
~ Peter Hopkins

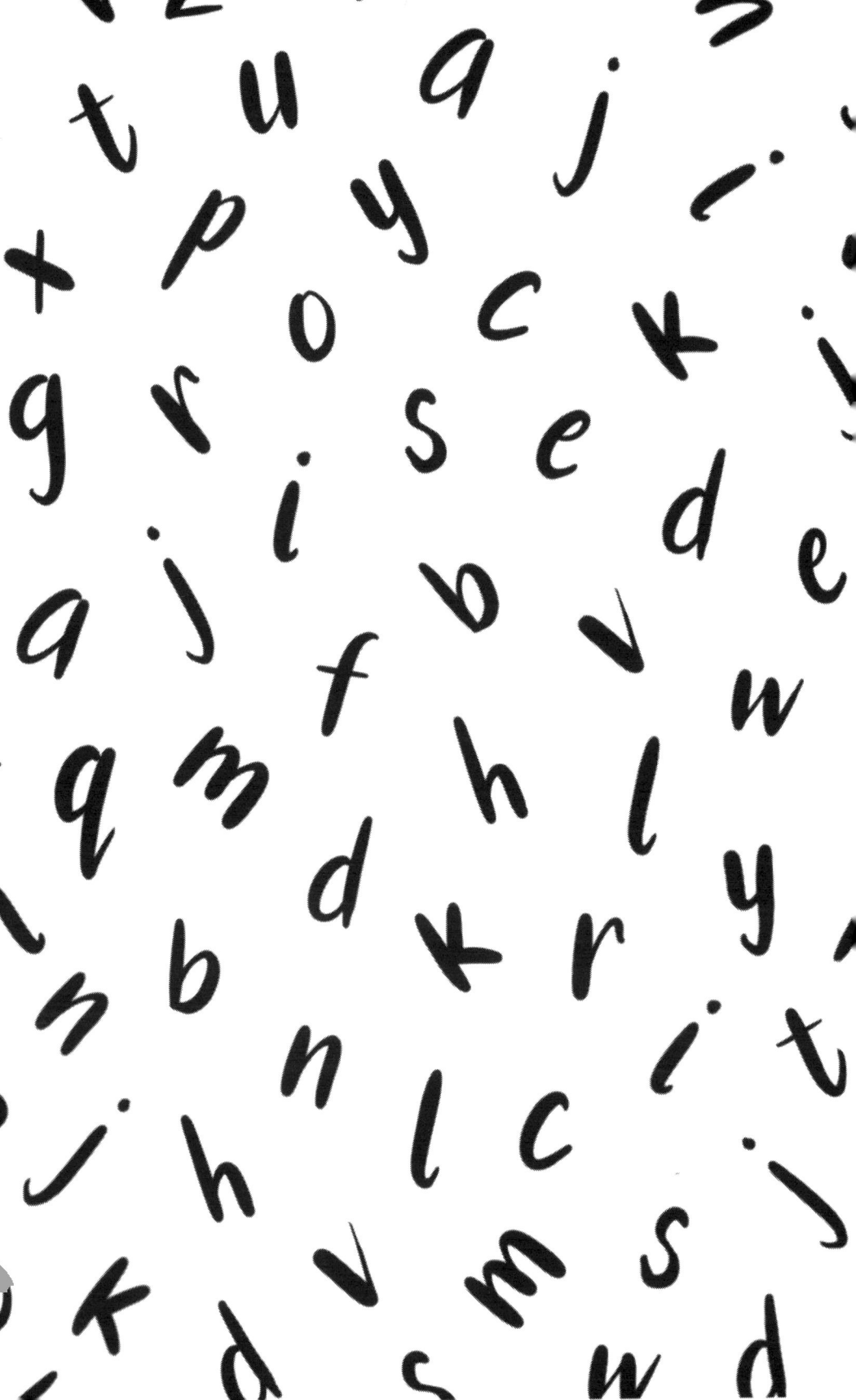

5

Curate your Blog

The term "blogging" can be quite ambiguous. Often times, we've seen #fblogs that dabble into a little bit of everything. If that's your vibe, then go for it. But make sure it doesn't appear haphazard and confusing for your readers. As long as you have determined your niche audience, curating your #fblog shouldn't be too difficult. Clarity is extremely important.

Make sure your #fblog is user-friendly and all genres within your blog (if any) are easily distinguished and easily accessible. How you do this is up to you, but the most common and my personal favorite is creating dedicated tabs on the home page leading to respective sections on your #fblog. If you are working with a Graphic Designer, provide them with a detailed *Design Brief* at the beginning of the journey. This will also help you find the right designer for your aesthetic needs. A *Design Brief* is where you specify what you are looking for in regards to your project. Colour specs, design inspirations, deadlines you are working with etc.

Just make sure you keep communication open with them throughout the design process, but don't bombard them with hundreds of changes either.

As long as you have been clear and detailed in your brief, your designer should be able to deliver what you are looking for.

6

Quality over Quantity

It is very important that you only post high quality content. If you're unsure about a post, save it in your drafts. Keep it for another day so you can look back and see if there is anything else you can add to make it better. Don't publish half thought out pieces of writing, because every post you publish either builds or breaks your #fblog. Many times, there can be a few posts we're really proud of, but as we become better #fbloggers, we realise that it might not have been our best work. There is no shame in sifting through old blog posts and delete, edit or hide old ones. It's a process, and you always want your best foot forward! Remember, you want to stand out in every sense!

"don't build
LINKS
build
RELATIONSHIPS"

— RAND FISHKIN

7

Market Your Brand

From the get go, you're at this alone and you need to get the word out about your #fblog. So what do you do? Market your brand on various Social Media platforms that I will be talking about in more detail in just a while. But, because you are "working for yourself", take your branding with you everywhere and shout it from the rooftops.

When you meet likeminded individuals, exchange your information. A little bit of effort will really go a long way.

Whether you are online or offline, talk about your #fblog and get people to pay it a visit. You arc your best billboard, so utilise any and every opportunity that presents itself to you.

5th Secret

"The camera is an instrument that teaches people how to see without a camera."
~ Dorothea Lange

"you don't take a PHOTOGRAPH you make it"

— ANSEL ADAMS

8

Images are everything...

Having beautiful images is one of the most important, if not *the* most important part of your #fblog. Having quality written content is definitely important, but if you have none at all or even low resolution images in your post, chances are you are not going to draw people in. You may even put them off completely!

Majority of people may not be fans of only reading, but everyone gets captured by well taken photographs or illustrations. We used to love picture books as kids, remember? Not much changes as we grow older, surprisingly!

Beautiful images are also very important in maintaining your *Instagram* account that supports your #fblog. I will be speaking more about *Instagram* later on in the book, but images you take for your #fblog are also part of your brand. They represent you as a #fblogger, so don't overlook them.

I don't want this to overwhelm you. Bloggers, especially #fbloggers always think they need to have the best DSLR camera on the market, but really, if you have a smartphone and good lighting, I'm pretty sure you can curate some beautiful images. Of course it's great if you DO have a DSLR with a good set of lenses, but essentially it's all about lighting, angles and editing that really give the subject life.

Be enterprising and find ways to get high quality results at relatively low budgets. With advancements in technology these days, it isn't that hard.

6th Secret

*Honesty is definitely
the best policy*

"honesty is the BEST policy"

— BENJAMIN FRANKLIN

9

Review Truthfully

Being honest for a #fblogger is absolutely essential in developing your relationship with your audience as well as brands alike. From what you write about a brand to your liasing with them; always be honest. Don't be biased in your opinion about them, their products or services because the audience can sniff it out very quickly. Having all good or all bad reviews on your #fblog is also not going to help you. Your approach needs to be balanced and carefully considered.

Explaining your experience from start to finish with the brand can also go a long way. Was the brand kind enough to send you the products at no cost to yourself? Was the item sent as a gift? Were you paid to write the review etc. As a #fblogger, you're the gateway to building or breaking customer trust and retention for brands, especially freshly emerging ones.

Always do your best to be as objective and honest as possible without coming across as someone stating faults just for the sake of being controversial, or for praising a brand just because you are being paid.

Whether you are paid or gifted, don't allow yourself to lose integrity when reviewing. Your reviews have an effect on the buying decisions of your readers. So, while #fblogging can be a lot of fun, there is a level of responsibility that comes with it.

10

Be Honest with Brands

Don't overbook yourself if you know you can't make the deadline for a review. This puts unnecessary strain on yourself, but it's also just bad business. Be honest about your schedule with the brands you're talking to.

A lot of times #fbloggers take on work that they don't have the time to fulfill. A few times, I have had #fbloggers commit to blogging but didn't deliver nor did they bother getting back in touch. Radio silence after committing to work is seen as unprofessional in any freelancing field; #fblogging is no different.

If you are unable to meet a certain deadline, it is good practice to let the brand know when the initial discussion is taking place. Brands can be flexible and they appreciate honest correspondence. You wouldn't like to be flaked out on and neither would they.

If for any reason, you are faced with extenuating circumstances that you couldn't have foreseen, don't hesitate to let the brand know as soon as you can. It can really help save your reputation in the industry. Sometimes life just takes over and it's okay.

But keep in mind not all brands will care unfortunately. If they refuse to work with you in the future despite you having a very valid reason for the delay, just take it with a grain of salt and move on.

7th Secret

Professionalism is Mandatory

" PROFESSIONALISM *means* CONSISTENCY *of quality*"

— FRANK TYGER

II

Be Professional

While #fblogging may be a "side hustle" for you right now or just a hobby, you will be dealing with people whose businesses are their "main hustle" and require you to be professional. The way you communicate with a brand is testament to your professionalism. Using words like "give me...", "send this...that" make you sound entitled to those products and it comes across as rude and arrogant. Do *not* do it.

The best initial mode of communication with brands is to be what I call *"friendly formal"*. Be kind and humble in your words without ordering them to send you products they spent time and money creating. If you're rude or come across as arrogant, they can choose at any time not to work with you now or ever again; and of course, the same goes for you. If you are not happy with the way a brand communicates with you, by all means, halt the "transaction", so to speak.

Also keep in mind that if brands ask to meet you in person or virtually via *Skype* at a specific time, make sure you are on time for the appointment. Being prompt shows you are a reliable person who is serious about their career as a #fblogger. And it is just good manners not to keep someone waiting, especially in a professional setting.

Professionlism is required in almost every field I can think of. Don't neglect it as a #fblogger, even if it is your "side hustle". You want to make a name for yourself, don't you?

12

Plan. Plan. Plan.

I've talked about this briefly before and not to sound repetitive, but meeting deadlines you commit to with brands is essential to the success of your #fblog. Not only does this create a positive relationship between you and the brand, it also helps you keep your #fblog afloat. If you don't set deadlines for yourself, chances are posts will not get done.

This is where creating a schedule for yourself is very important. Planning out posts in advance really helps with delivering your reviews on time. Often, you just want to blog for yourself; talk about a particular product that caught your eye, or maybe you have a weekly series. Scheduling and planning are your best friends when it comes to

#fblogging. Scheduling is even more important to implement especially if it is your "side hustle".

Choose between a physical planner that you handwrite your schedule and meetings in, or apps like the Calendar app on your device, Calendars 5, Pocket Schedule or others similar to these. Whatever method you choose, the key thing is to stay organised.

Soon enough you will find a rhythm and scheduling posts will be very natural. It will become a mandatory process for you to stay productive. Some of you may find this a meticulous process, but, it really keeps you from procrastination.

Whether you want a traditional planner or a virtual one, choose which you feel most comfortable with and you'll definitely see results.

8th Secret

Consistency is the "key to success."
"Anotha one...and anotha one"
~ DJ Khaled

13

Be Consistent

To really make a go of anything, you need to be consistent and persistent. Consistency in any action allows you to create a habit, and when it is paired with #fblogging it helps build your audience. If your posts are random and on a monthly or yearly basis, needless to say, it really won't take off. This is where you will discover what a Holy Grail planning your posts really is.

Remember when you were in school or university? You had a syllabus and deadlines for papers and projects to be handed in on a set date and time. If we didn't have these dates that were set in stone, you wouldn't have gotten anything done. The only difference

Creating a schedule for yourself and sticking to it will do wonders. This is not to say that your schedule is set in stone, like your school or uni days. If you are having an off day, or its one of those days you're not too happy with your post; feel free to skip it. Like I said before, your readers want quality not quantity. So learn how to balance your life with your "side hustle" but don't burn yourself out.

9th Secret

Your blog is your portfolio

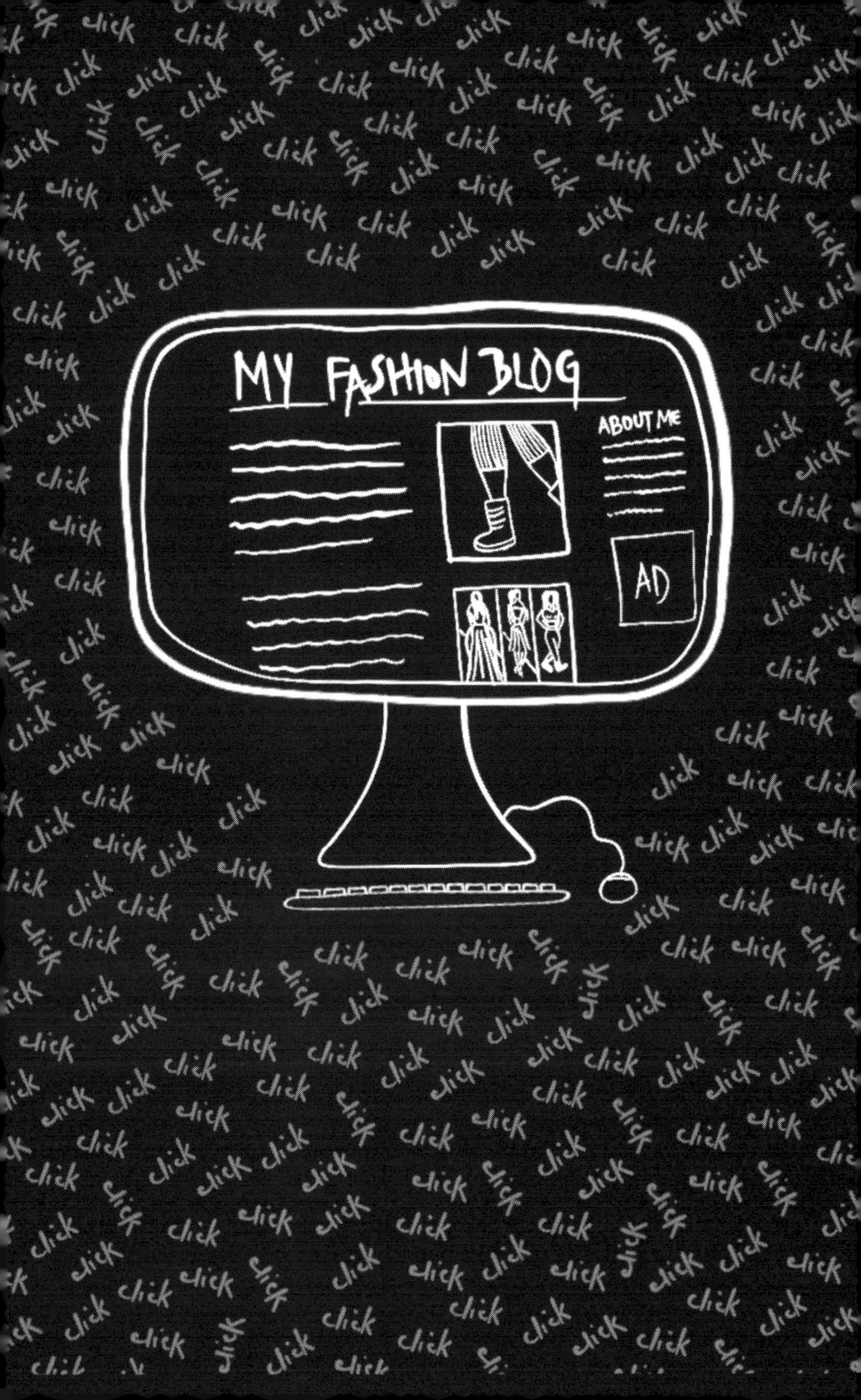
MY FASHION BLOG
ABOUT ME
AD
click

14

Building your Portfolio

Naturally, when you first create your blog, you are not going to be contacted by any brands. This is where it is up to you to begin curating the content on your #fblog and review products that you would like to see on your blog in the future. The initial step to building your #fblog portfolio is to spend your own money in order to review products.

A very handy tip is for you to really find a gap in the market and see what other #fbloggers *aren't* doing and you feel it is something the community is in need of. It can be a diamond in the rough at first, but if you keep at it long enough, you may have a real gem in your hands.

Another way to build your portfolio of blog posts is to join online communities that are created specifically for #fbloggers to review new brands and their products. These are called gifting communities where brands "gift" their products that are worth a lot of money in exchange for exposure.

Now, let me warn you. You may be tempted to get carried away when you see "free" things. Don't let it happen. I will talk more about the best ethics to employ when finding work through gifting communities later on in the book.

Once you have a good range of blog posts, you can begin contacting bigger brands that do have the capacity to pay you for writing a review for them. But they will only want to work with you if you have presented your #fblog in an appealing manner. So keep that in mind.

10th Secret

Rome wasn't built in a day and neither will your readership

" *little*
BY
little,
a little
BECOMES
a lot "

— TANZANIAN PROVERB

15

Slow and Steady

Don't get impatient. It's really easy to, but try not to.

"Rome wasn't built in a day, but they were laying bricks every hour." ~ John Heywood.

If you put in the grind, you will get noticed eventually. Don't get disheartened by the fact that you aren't getting hundreds of views in your first week of #fblogging. Success in anything takes time. Work on your "brand identity" and "brand recognition" in the early days of your #fblog. This means you need to work on getting the word out about yourself and your #fblog. This will consequently be a way for you to pull in a readership. Some methods to create "brand recognition" is through networking, online and offline. You'll find out more about this shortly.

Remember, baby steps. But consistent ones!

Just keep building. Just keep building.
sang Dory
sssshh yes, that is what she sang!

11th Secret

Social Media platforms are important, but don't spread yourself too thin

"the internet is becoming THE TOWN SQUARE for the GLOBAL VILLAGE of tomorrow"

— BILL GATES

16

Online Real Estate

So if you are a complete novice to #fblogging and are struggling to figure out how and where to set up your #fblog, here's the scoop.

There are a number of host sites you can house your #fblog on; the ones that give the best impression in my opinion are *WordPress* and/or *Blogspot*. Both of these platforms offer free services where you choose from a selection of free themes to create your website. The only catch here is that your URL will be

"YOURFBLOG.WORDPRESS.COM" or "YOURFBLOG.BLOGSPOT.COM".

There are a few #fbloggers who choose to be

only on *Tumblr*. In my opinion, you could have a *Tumblr* that compliments your official #fblog, but not as a stand alone. If you have the cash to spare, you can purchase your own unique domain name and host your #fblog on a server with *GoDaddy* and/or *NamesCo*. This allows you to create your entire #fblog from scratch using *Wordpress.org* and create the site using coding. Many times this task is hired out.

This is a great option, but requires a monthly payment which may or may not be something you want to invest in at the start. Not to mention the cost of the coder if you choose to hire help. It's absolutely brilliant if you can, but if it's not financially possible, don't sweat it. All I'd suggest is you purchase your desired domain name in advance, which is an annual payment. You want to do this so it isn't snapped up by someone else before you create your custom #fblog.

17

Social Media Queen

In terms of social media, the most effective places to have your presence is *Twitter, Instagram, Snapchat* and *Tumblr* may work for some. You could choose to have a *Facebook* page, but I really don't feel that's where you will get much traction.

For the most part, *Twitter, Instagram* and/or *Snapchat* should be your best friends as a #fblogger. *Snapchat* is like "micro vlogging" where the content posted remains for 24 hours and is then deleted forever. You can use this platform to connect with your audience in a different way that is more engaging and personal by recording your experience at fashion events or your recent hauls.

I'll go into more detail in the upcoming pages about these platforms. But generally, use *Twitter* to promote your blog posts and connect with other #fbloggers and beauty bloggers.

Instagram exhibits your #fblogging photography skills, as it is an extension of your blogging portfolio in an image gallery. *Instagram* also rolled out *Insta Stories* in 2016 which is nearly identical to *Snapchat's* platform. The only differences are being able to *live stream* as well as potentially a bigger audience who watch your stories based on your follower count.

YouTube is also a platform you can choose to explore, but remember not to spread yourself too thin.

As a #fblogger, see which platforms give you the best results and press on!

18

Twitter

When it comes to Social Media platforms, *Twitter* is a #fbloggers best friend. Why, you ask? *Twitter* is where you can reach your readership by posting links to your blog posts. One of the best ways to also come into contact with others in your field, is by using hashtags like "#fblogger", "#fblog", "#fbloggersUK" etc. When you search under these hashtags, you can make some very interesting contacts who you can collaborate with.

The best thing about the #fblogger community is the amount of support that is given to each other. Chances are, your posts will be retweeted which can increase the chances of your exposure to their followers

Don't forget to reciprocate the gesture; this builds good will and can also create real life friendships.

Another very useful aspect of being on *Twitter* is taking part in "Twitter Chats". Those specifically that are created for #fbloggers. Some of the most participated chats can be found using the hashtags "#fbloggerchat", "#chattybees" etc, and are normally 30 minutes to an hour long. The duration each chat is held and at what time, is completely the chat hosts decision and is advertised a few days in advance or in their *Twitter* bios.

Twitter chats are excellent as the hosts have prepared a specific theme for that week. Thought provoking questions are asked that generally help one reflect on their journey thus far. It is not rare that you leave the chat with more information than you came in with as well as feeling a lot better about your decision to blog. It is nice to talk to others who are on a similar journey as you are.

When it comes to tweeting your blog post, a lot of #fbloggers also throw in other hashtags that are not necessarily their niche, but can help gain more readers, like: "#bbloggers" (beauty bloggers) and/or #lbloggers" (lifestyle bloggers) amongst others. Use hashtags you find the most engagement from. Don't overcrowd your tweet with hashtags because that just looks cluttered and a little desperate. A maximum of 3 hashtags is a happy medium.

Twitter is an excellent way to engage with your audience and acts as virtual networking. It is a must-have for anyone looking to venture into #fblogging.

19

Instagram

As mentioned previously, *Instagram* is definitely a necessity for every #fblogger. Why? Because it allows you to show case your gorgeous photography, products and aesthetic all in one concise location. Besides this, you are very likely to find readers and loyal followers of your #fblog based on how you present your *Instagram* account. Not to mention that brands definitely look at all aspects of *your* brand aesthetic to see whether or not you would fit theirs.

Some insider secrets on having a gorgeous *Instagram* feed are (1) considering the contents of your images and their placement within a 3 x 3 grid and (2) creating a colour theme that transitions seamlessly.

So you might be wondering, how exactly do I make my feed look so put together? This is where your editing skills come into play, as well as your photographic skills. Firstly you need to choose what kind of vibe you want your feed to have; colourful, monochrome, subdued, or maybe you could use the colour scheme of your brand and edit your pictures accordingly using colour filters.

You could choose to edit your images on *Photoshop*, but majority of fashionistas choose to edit their images on their devices using apps like *VSCO*, *Snapseed* or directly on *Instagram*. You can play with the hues, temperature, brightness, highlights, shadows and contrast of the image for your desired effect.

Once edited, think about the image on an individual basis, and also consider it within a grid with other images you have already uploaded. Does it explain what you do? Does it follow the colour theme of your Instagram feed? Your #fblog branding colours? If not, can you edit further so that it will? These are all things to consider when working towards an exciting and engaging *Instagram* feed.

Why is it important? Because on first glance, everyone's account appears as a grid. Most of the time, people scroll through your feed initially to understand your vibe. If an image strikes them, they will click on it and engage liking and/or commenting on it. So make sure it is visually enticing.

To help make this process a little easier, there are some apps that can help with this, like *Planoly or Preview - Feed Design and Schedule.* These apps assist you in planning your feed before you commit to the images on *Instagram.* This saves you a lot of uploading and deleting before your followers see your images. They are really great tools that ease up the slightly meticulous task of keeping your feed 'matching'. It can seem a little daunting at first, but practise makes better.

For inspiration, look at the feeds of other #fbloggers and see what they are doing. Find what works for you, and hit the ground running.

Don't feel you have to do what everyone else is doing. In fact, *don't*. Find your unique voice when it comes to visuals and I am sure you will find *your* audience.

20

YouTube

YouTube is also another avenue #fbloggers have at their disposal. I suggest starting a *YouTube* channel once you have established a loyal readership on your #fblog. At least this way, you know there is an audience for the content you are pushing out and can be successful. With a *YouTube* channel, you can then take your product reviews to video. A lot of #fbloggers choose to have their blog and *YouTube* channel coincide with one another. They do this by giving you snippets of information on the product in their videos and then redirect you to their #fblog for more information.

In my experience, the fewer social media platforms you're on, the more concentrated and curated your content can be. It will allow you to focus more on a few platforms you can post on regularly, as opposed to four or five where you post once or twice a week or even less.

Fewer platforms will help your audience know where you are at all times and will have them coming back for more. Choose at least one or two platforms you are most comfortable with and stick with them.

21

Live Streaming
&
Micro Vlogging

Live Streaming is also another platform some people choose to use in order to engage with their readers. *Periscope, Facebook Live and Instagram Live* are some of the platforms you may choose to use for Live Streaming. But you need to measure for yourself whether this is an absolute necessity for your #fblogging journey.

The only time these platforms would really be beneficial is when you have a really dedicated following and they are hooked on to you. Live Streaming can make you appear more personable and feel connected to your audience on a different level. So explore this option if you are feeling adventurous.

This idea is really interchangeable with *Snapchat* and *Instagram Stories* as well. The benefit of these platforms is that you can "curate" the content you are posting via micro vlogging, but you are able to reach your audience at any time during the 24 hours of uploading the content. If you are not familiar with these platforms, any content posted is deleted after 24 hours. It just depends on what platform you feel the easiest in using and which platform your readers are already using.

The only way you will really figure which is best is through trial and error. Who knows, you might just get readers from these avenues. Always try. If it doesn't work to your advantage, don't be afraid to drop it and move on.

22

Don't be overwhelmed

There are several other social media platforms you may choose to be a part of. The issue is, there is always going to be something new. What you need to decide is, "Will it work for me?" "Is it going to help me build my audience?" "Will it help me connect with my audience?" "Can I commit to this?" These are all important questions to ask. If you feel you can, go for it!

Once you do commit to certain platforms, make sure you are always in tune with the changes the developers make. This way you will be able to use the platform to your advantage, and make the most of it. It's very easy to fall behind on these changes if you don't make a conscious decision to keep up tweaks and updates.

Visit the technology section on *BBC* or other similar websites to be the first to know.

12th Secret

Build Relationships and Attract Brands

23

Network

So, you've got your Social Media platforms down and are making good progress, so what do you need 'networking' for? How is it going to help your #fblogger journey? I already touched upon using *Twitter* as an avenue for *virtual networking*, so what am I talking about here?

Well, just as any other business, it is important to get a feel for the industry that you are in. Meeting other like minded people in real life is very rewarding. You have the opportunity to spread the word about yourself, and also pick up some new tips and tricks you weren't aware of before. It is also an excuse to just wind down and have a little bit of fun! Going at it alone can be nice since you can make up your own work schedule, but trust me when I say that it gets lonely; fast.

There are always #fblogger networking events going around in London (and most probably in a lot of cities). This is where trusty *Twitter* comes in handy. Look through the usual hashtags I mentioned before (and others) to see if there are any events going on near you. For people outside of London and if you have a group of #fbloggers you already know, why not host an event yourself and get the ball rolling if it isn't already being done? There is no harm in being a leader in such situations!

Alot of the events that I have come across, the organiser of these events generally brings together goody bags with products from brands that have been contacted to specifically participate for the #fblogger event. This is a way for small and big brands alike, to get some exposure as the #fbloggers at these events will go home and blog about the event. Most of the the time, they will go into quite a bit of detail by taking pictures of products they received in the goody bag and drum up some hype for the brands involved.

At the same time, this is also very useful for new #fbloggers to create content and get noticed by brands involved and otherwise.

Anything and everything can help. So do give real life networking a try! You will *not* regret it.

"the law of
BRAND
attraction"

— MiA ROSE

24

Build Rapport With Brands

If you take your #fblogging seriously and implement the secrets and tips I have given you so far, chances are you will end up building good relationships with the brands that you have worked with and attract new ones. Lets call it the "Law of Brand Attraction". This is important because it provides credibility for your brand, gives you exposure as well as the brands. Additionally, it is just a good feeling when those you are working with are happy with the content you provide and actually want to work with you again. It is a fail proof formula to success if you choose to stick to it.

They could even offer you paid work if what you deliver is to their liking. This is why I said don't neglect "unpaid" work.

Just because there wasn't an exchange of cash on your initial encounter, it doesn't mean there wasn't an exchange of a product for a service. I will go into more detail about "unpaid work" later on in the book. But think of it this way; these projects as an "audition" of sorts.

How? I will explain in just a little bit.

13th Secret

Make an appearance on other fashion blogs and YouTube channels "if you're only blogging on your own BLOG, you're doing it WRONG"

— ANDY CRESTODINA

25

Guest Blog

Besides writing for posts for your own #fblog, in yet another method to gain recognition, is to Guest Blog. This is where you write fashion pieces for another #fbloggers site. Their audience gets a chance to see your work and if they like it, they can start following your #fblog and other various social media platforms. Obviously it is a good idea to have other #fbloggers write for yours as well. It switches up the content and adds more elements of interest.

This is where your networking online and offline comes into play. If you make good connections, you can organise guest blogging for one another. Be creative with your approach.

"guest blogging is a process that can INCREASE your REACH, INFLUENCE and WEB TRAFFIC"

— ANNALIESE HENWOOD

26

Guest Blog for Brands

Following on from the previous point, you can also find yourself guest blogging for brands that are looking to collaborate with #fbloggers. These brands can range from small to big brands that are looking to feature unique #fbloggers with content that matches their vibe.

It never hurts to reach out to brands to see if they would be interested. I have worked with and featured a lot of #fbloggers on the *KryptikRose™* #fblog. It gave new and interesting content for my customers, and it consequently gave the #fbloggers I worked with, exposure. I always made sure I gave credit where it was due and included their #fblog URL as well as any other social media platforms they wanted readers to connect with.

Indie brands are usually more friendly and are also more receptive to content providers. You both are able to build your audiences at the same time, so it's really a great collaboration.

Again, these are all methods with which you can build your #fblogger portfolio and continue to create brand awareness and eventually brand recognition, which should lead to a loyal following.

14th Secret

Integrity shines through

"do what is
RIGHT
not
what is
EASY"

— ROY T. BENNETT

27

Integrity as a Fashion Blogger

I have always been an advocate for giving a voice to new #fbloggers that are starting up. One complaint that I often came across from girls I worked with was that, no brand was willing to work with them because they were so new and didn't have a massive following. Even for some girls who had worked very hard on their brand, faced the same situation because they did not have a following in the hundreds of thousands yet.

Yes, having a large audience is an absolute asset for fashion or make up brands looking to make a mark, but it is also important that they are working with people who are just as dedicated and fit with their brand, regardless of the #fbloggers audience count. This is an excellent way to create life long business relationships between yourself as a #fblogger and brands in fashion or cosmetics when you work together. Your integrity as a #fblogger can be seen from a mile off if you are dedicated and putting in the work.

At the same time, there are a group of girls who expect products and payment, but their websites left much to be desired. They don't have branding of any sort, nor is their content linked with any kind of niche. Their content is poorly executed with low resolution images. They literally blog about anything and everything. These kinds of blogs can be good as a personal one, but for someone who is looking to make #fblogging a career? Absolutely not! This is why it is important to find your niche and work within it. Once you are clear on what you want to write about, you can set things in motion and brands will most probably be more receptive to you.

Also, don't ask for a product to be sent to you and then NOT write a blog post for it at all! That is highly unprofessional and unfair. It has happened one or two times and needless to say, I never worked with those #fbloggers again. Some also said that they "lost" the items. Whether or not this was true, if something like this happens, let the brand know and don't leave them hanging. Don't have them chase you down months later wondering where their blog post is. It just reflects poorly on your integrity as a #fblogger and wastes their time and money.

Integrity is everything when it comes to building relationships of any kind. Same goes for professional #fblogging ones.

" *you are what*
you do,
NOT
what you say
you'll do "

— C.G JUNG

28

Integrity as a Brand

Please don't feel that my opinion is only one sided. Of course, brands should also deal with their customers and #fbloggers with integrity as well. Being available as soon as possible when they are contacted about a package, answering any and all questions that they are asked by the #fblogger in regards to their company and their products, communicating in a professional manner as well as sending items that are of good quality.

Production malfunctions do happen, and sometimes a product that is sent off can be faulty or damaged. Sometimes the product is fine when it is dispatched from the company warehouse, but gets damaged along the way. Now, this is where it is up to the brand on how they want to approach things. Some can offer to send a replacement, something that I have happily done. Others can choose not to, but it can leave a bad after taste. Of course it is not in our control what happens during transport, and many times despite our best efforts of packing the products, things can still go wrong.

If they choose to refuse to send a replacement, they are absolutely within their rights. However, if they do send a replacement, it just makes for better relationship building in the long run and a better "customer experience". If they care about Customer Service, they will send a replacement!

So what did you learn from this section?

Never let brands bully you, and don't bully the brands either. Mutual respect is the absolute best!

15th Secret

Building trust as a professional

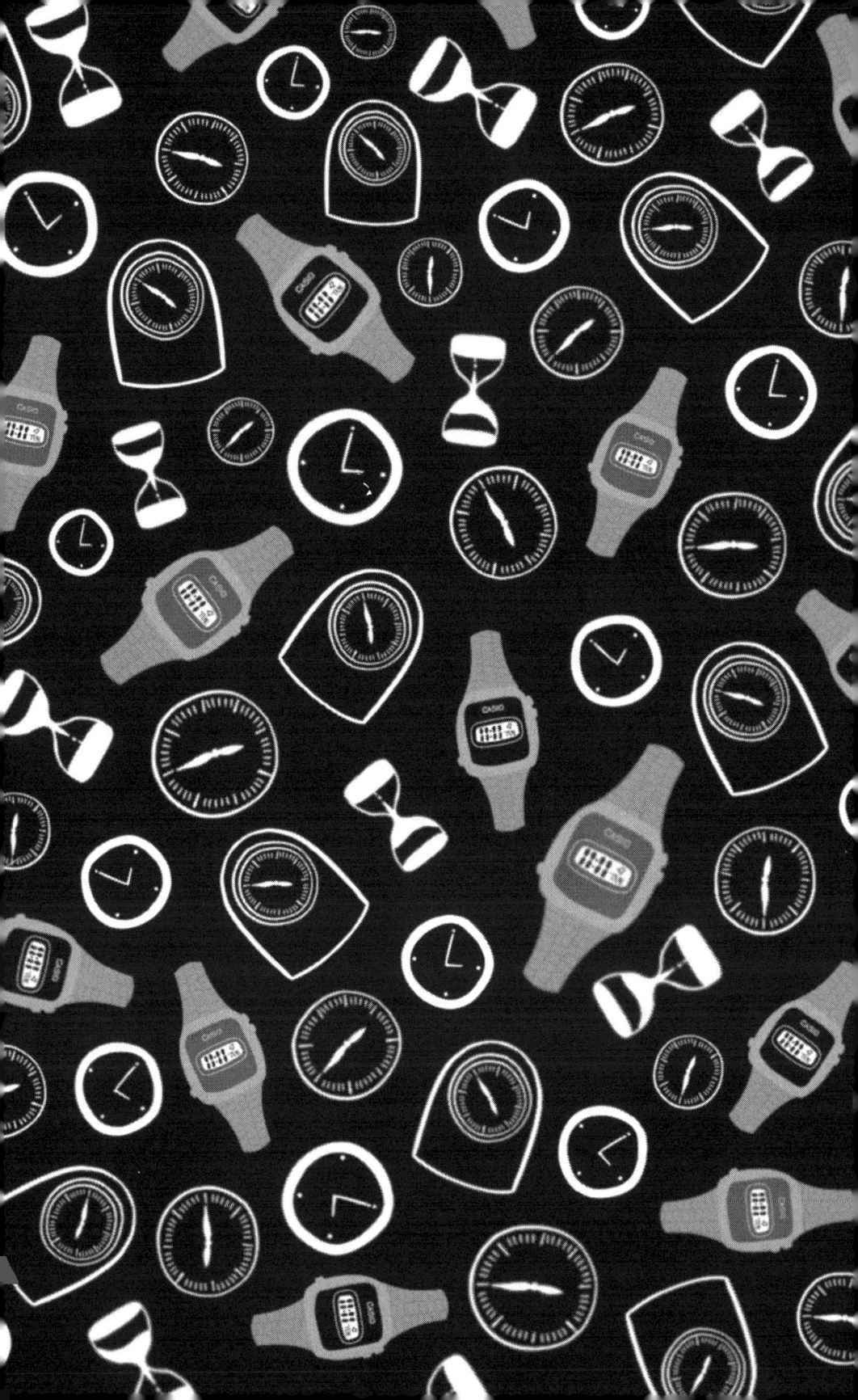

29

Building trust with Brands

The only way you are able to actually build trust with brands is to deliver what you have promised. This is where your integrity as a "brand" and #fblogger really are instrumental. When you deliver what you have promised, when you promised it, is when a trusting and positive relationship is built between brands and #fbloggers.

If for any reason, you are faced with extenuating circumstances that will cause you to be unable to provide content on the deadline, contact the brand as soon as possible to let them know. Don't wait for them to chase you after the deadline has passed. Even if you have a valid reason, it doesn't do you any favours to have left the brand you were working with hanging. So make sure you do let them know what is going on.

I have worked with some #fbloggers who unfortunately had certain health conditions that crept up at any given time. Some were professional in letting me know about the delays and of course, it was understandable. Others were not and needed to be chased down.

Maybe they felt embarrassed and did not know how to approach a brand about a matter like this. It is practice to mention certain health limitations in your initial correspondence with the brand just to get it out there. Be open and true to who you are, and share it with the brands you are working with. I am sure they will really appreciate it and you will build a trusting relationship with them.

16th Secret

Income is nearly everyone's end goal, but don't become greedy "there is no substitute for HARD WORK. there is no such thing as OVERNIGHT SUCCESS or EASY MONEY"

— HENRY SY

30

Don't Knock Unpaid Work

If you are looking to get into #fblogging to earn "easy money" straight away, then look away. If you don't have a serious passion for fashion, or don't have a knack for creating written content and images regularly and on a schedule, I will be honest, you probably won't be able to make #fblogging your actual profession.

As with anything, #fblogging requires a lot of ground work, a lot of *hard* work and patience. If you put in the hours and the effort to create beautiful content that people enjoy reading, *yes*, you will eventually grab the attention of the crème de la crème in the fashion industry.

As a newbie #fblogger, you are going to be

creating posts based off of products you have purchased yourself. If your curation is eye catching, brands may approach you with a prospect of reviewing their product, but would not pay you. This exchange is not a bad deal, especially as a new #fblogger. You are essentially being paid in kind, not money. You receive a product for free, which allows you to "build your portfolio" as a blogger. Don't refuse a review just because you are not getting physical money in your bank account with only two or three blog posts in your portfolio. Humble beginnings are in the past of anyone who succeeds.

If you deliver content the brand likes and is happy with the way you communicated with them, who knows, you could become a regular #fblogger these brands reach out to every time they launch a new product and actually earn money! Don't knock it 'til you try it.

31

Don't Be Greedy with Freebies

A really great way for #fbloggers to connect with brands is through communities that are created specifically for "gifting" #fbloggers. *Gifting* is the term used when brands are sending products to #fbloggers for review without paying them an additional fee. While this is an amazing way for both brands and #fbloggers to achieve *brand awareness*, it can easily go pear shaped if care is not taken.

It's easy for some to get carried away when they approach these platforms solely to receive free products. In my experience, majority of the girls I worked with were professional and produced absolutely brilliant blog posts. Having said that, there were unfortunately a handful of #fbloggers who "loved" and wanted a number of products, but would not purchase simply because they thought they could get it all for free. Remember, do not take advantage of brands and these gifting sites. Work with the guidelines the websites have specified or what the brands are offering. If you ask for multiple products because you like them and simply do not want to pay and don't post high quality content, know for a fact that you will be blacklisted.

As mentioned before, the products sent out for review are at no cost to the #fblogger, but the brand is parting with potential money earners. It is only fair that the exchange is met with high quality content production. I am not even talking about whether they liked or didn't like the product. It is about the delivery.

17th Secret

How to Earn Money as a #fblogger

32

Affiliate Marketing

As a beginner #fblogger, you *can* potentially earn some money with *Affiliate Marketing.* This is when you either host ads on your #fblog or post links of various brands that offer affiliate marketing options. What many books and articles do not make clear is that, the way in which you earn through *affiliate marketing*, is based on the number of clicks on the ad or link; and the number of potential clicks is based on how much traffic you get on your site. If you have 5-10 visitors a day, you can understand that your earnings will not be very high, nor help you keep the lights on.

But, having said that, you can definitely learn the ropes of *affiliate marketing* and set it up on your #fblog fairly early on.

In fact, I encourage it. I just want you to know that chances are, you will only see real monetary gain when you start getting a lot of traffic on your blog and those visitors click on the affiliate links.

Very logical, to be honest. If you have it all set up early on, once traffic starts to pick up on your #fblog, you will be raking the money in!

33

Earning with Blog Posts

Once you have built a respectable #fblogging portfolio and are getting thousands of visitors to your #fblog daily and/or monthly, you can confidently start looking for paid work. When you are at this stage of your #fblogging career, take the time to create a *Media Kit*. This contains information about your #fblog, who your target audience is, and should include screen grabs of the traffic you receive on your #fblog. This is important to have because it is easy for anyone to "fake it". So showing evidence of the traffic you receive is absolutely necessary and valuable.

Within this *Media Kit*, include your rates for posts and reviews. You can even include a little snippet where you offer flexibility and can tailor your prices around the wants and needs of the brand. This helps you earn money and makes you a likeable #fblogger.

You can even include the names and logos of other well known publications you have written for. This will exemplify your *'prestige'* and help brands understand why they should pay you for a review.

Take your time in creating your *Media Kit* because this is the document you will be sending brands when they approach you for a review. Make sure it is succinct but captures the essence of your brand really well. Just make sure you come across as approachable and willing to be flexible with packages as opposed to being very rigid.

You haven't made it just yet, so its probably best to keep that kind of attitude to the side. Once you reach Kim K's status, then go for it.

34

Brand Ambassador

Being a *"Brand Ambassador"* or *"Brand Representative"* means that you represent a brand on your #fblog, social media platforms as well as any events that you go to. These could be magazine events, fashion weeks and other similar events. This is also another way that you can possibly earn money and/or can earn you *"brand recognition"*. It depends on your contract and the terms that both parties agree to.

Often times the brand you are representing will post about your latest news on their various social media platforms. This is amazing for both you and the brand to create hype about each other.

35

Collaborate with a Brand

Once you gain well deserved popularity, after putting in all the hard work, and you find a brand that has the aesthetic, style and ethics that you endorse, you can potentially collaborate with them. Collaborating with a brand is when you work with the brand to create a product or collection.

We are beginning to see this a lot on *YouTube*, where *YouTube* personalities who may or may not be beauty gurus, get to collaborate with cosmetic brands like Lilly Singh's collab with *Smashbox* or Bunny a.k.a. GRAV3YARDGIRL's collab with *Tarte*. There is no reason why the same cannot happen with an established #fblogger or beauty blogger.

If one collaboration is successful, chances are you will have the opportunity to create more collections with them! If you have the drive and the willingness to persevere, anything is possible!

18th Secret

Analytics

"what gets MEASURED, gets MANAGED"

— PETER DRUCKER

36

Observe and Adjust

As you are creating, curating and building your blog, you are also working to market yourself. All of the steps mentioned here are ways in which you are marketing your brand; whether it is through your own social media platforms, guest blogging on other #fbloggers sites or for other brands. The end goal is always to try and attain traffic to *your* #fblog.

Monitoring the analytics of your #fblog is something that will be very valuable for you as you progress on the journey to becoming a successful #fblogger. You can get a better look at the demographic your content is *actually* reaching. Sometimes it can be completely different to who you intended, but now you understand exactly who likes your work and where they are located. You can often also see where they have found your #fblog from; whether it was a Google search, or it was a click from Twitter, Facebook or another #fblog.

Most analytics sections of blogs show you which posts are more popular than others and how many people have clicked on the article. This is a good way for you to understand what kind of content your audience likes, so you can create more of it.

Observe the analytics and adjust your #fblogging strategies accordingly to maximise the return. If you are consistent with the kind of content your audience likes, they are more likely to share the content with their family and friends. So never neglect the analytics section by thinking it is just numbers; these numbers *are* your "bread and butter".

19th Secret

Take a Break

37

You Need Your Beauty Sleep

So, I know I have been talking a lot about all the secrets to becoming a #fblogger and how to attract brands on your journey. I have talked about the *do's* and *don'ts* when it comes to working with brands and yes, the only way to success is the *"go, go, go"* attitude.

But...

Knowing when you need to take a break, or knowing your cut off time each day is equally important in the secrets to becoming a successful #fblogger. Going hard, all day every day sounds ambitious, and it is, but it isn't smart. If you go down this route, you will burn out soon enough and crash. Crashing is *not* your best friend, believe me I know. So learn to manage your "work hours" well in advance. And get a good nights sleep! A girl needs to look and feel her best. Getting a good nights sleep is the first key to that.

Don't pull an all nighter, struggling to push out a blog post if it is not time sensitive. Shut your devices, and relax, read a book, watch Netflix or just go to sleep. You might feel inspired in the morning after having slept on it. If you are still stuck, maybe give it a miss altogether. Writers block is natural and happens to the best of us, specifically when we are creating new content that is not a review.

You *are* allowed to take a day or two off. But, when you do, make sure to keep the activity going on your social media platforms and #fblog with scheduled posts. No one will be the wiser, unless you want your audience to know!

20th Secret

You Made It!

38

You've Made It

Woohoo girl, you made it! Through consistency, dedication and perseverance, you finally made it! You have an amazing following who is your tribe and you've made waves in the fashion industry! I am so proud of you!

Your phone is ringing off the hook and your emails are literally overflowing. You're writing posts and doing photoshoots and you have projects you are working on left, right and centre. Ah! You can't handle this all on your own anymore! So what do you do?

Turn the page and I will tell you!

"we rise by
LIFTING
others"

— ROBERT INGERSOLL

39

Build a Team

Here is when you start building your team with like minded people, but with different perspectives. They say opposites attract, and this isn't necessarily only exclusive to your love life. Build your team with people who understand your aesthetic and your drive, but who are not simply "yes men or women". They will participate, they will brainstorm and help you take your brand from great to awesome!

Delegate, delegate, delegate.

When you have built your team, delegating is your saving grace. It frees up so much time and only the most important tasks are on *your* schedule; creating content for your

#fblog and other tasks that require *you* to be there.

The best action you can take is create more leaders within your team that can help you take your brand from amazing to galactic heights! Believe me, you will never regret this decision and this will happen naturally when your workload starts to get unbearable.

So, get the normalcy back into your life. After all, being a girl boss doesn't have to come at the expense of your sanity and personal life.

You *can* have it all!

40

Evolve

Any profession requires you to evolve and adapt to new surroundings, but it is at a much faster pace in the fashion industry. As an #fblogger you will see yourself evolve throughout your career and adapt to the latest trends in not just the fashion trends, but in how you communicate with your audience.

If you're rigid and stubborn, you will become dated extremely fast in the fashion scene, since trends change and evolve at super sonic speed. Explore different avenues in delivering your message. Who knows, you could even eventually evolve into creating your own line of products if you choose to go down that path.

The sky is *not* the limit.

The only one who creates limitations is *you* for *yourself.* Believe in yourself as I believe in you.

I AM SURE YOU WILL GO PLACES.

Best of luck girl, you've got this!

Much love,

"i am NOT afraid. i was BORN to do this"

— JOAN OF ARC

#FBlogg
blogging
#fblch
FUN
vlogging
fashion
hauls
contest
INSTAGRAM
what I
#OUTF
H & M
fashion
haul
clothing
milan fashion w
#streetstyle
INSTA
SOHO
#FOTD
COSMO
fashion
#diy
shoe
SOHO
NYFW
review products
guest blog
WORDPR
highstreet

blogger

Styling

wearing

Celebrity

KR

LFW - LONDON FASHION WEEK

Street wear

FASHION

YouTube

lookbook

ART network

FREEBIE

GOAL

Chanel #5

#FBlog

#fblog

#hion

fhion

TWITTER

FACEBOOK

collab

TOPSHOP

99er

#MCM

STREET

#

#beechat

affiliate

Printed in Poland
by Amazon Fulfillment
Poland Sp. z o.o., Wrocław